The Data Visualization Sketchbook

Sara Miller McCune founded SAGE Publishing in 1965 to support the dissemination of usable knowledge and educate a global community. SAGE publishes more than 1000 journals and over 800 new books each year, spanning a wide range of subject areas. Our growing selection of library products includes archives, data, case studies and video. SAGE remains majority owned by our founder and after her lifetime will become owned by a charitable trust that secures the company's continued independence.

Los Angeles | London | New Delhi | Singapore | Washington DC | Melbourne

The Data Visualization Sketchbook

Stephanie D. H. Evergreen

Evergreen Data & Evaluation, LLC

Los Angeles | London | New Delhi
Singapore | Washington DC | Melbourne

FOR INFORMATION:

SAGE Publications, Inc.
2455 Teller Road
Thousand Oaks, California 91320
E-mail: order@sagepub.com

SAGE Publications Ltd.
1 Oliver's Yard
55 City Road
London EC1Y 1SP
United Kingdom

SAGE Publications India Pvt. Ltd.
B 1/I 1 Mohan Cooperative Industrial Area
Mathura Road, New Delhi 110 044
India

SAGE Publications Asia-Pacific Pte. Ltd.
18 Cross Street #10-10/11/12
China Square Central
Singapore 048423

Printed in the United States of America

ISBN: 978-1-5443-5100-1

This book is printed on acid-free paper.

Certified Chain of Custody
Promoting Sustainable Forestry
www.sfiprogram.org
SFI-01268

SFI label applies to text stock

Acquisitions Editor: Helen Salmon
Editorial Assistant: Megan O'Heffernan
Marketing Manager: Shari Countryman
Production Editor: Veronica Stapleton Hooper
Copy Editor: Rachel Keith
Typesetter: C&M Digitals (P) Ltd.
Proofreader: Dennis W. Webb
Cover Designer: Scott Van Atta

19 20 21 22 23 10 9 8 7 6 5 4 3 2 1

/// CONTENTS

Dr. Stephanie D. H. Evergreen is a sought-after speaker, designer, and researcher. She is best known for bringing a research-based approach to helping others better communicate their work through more effective graphs, slides, and reports. She holds a PhD from Western Michigan University in interdisciplinary research, which included a dissertation on the extent of graphic design use in written data reporting. Dr. Evergreen has trained audiences worldwide through keynote presentations and workshops for clients such as Verizon, Head Start, American Institutes for Research, Brookings Institute, the Ad Council, Boys and Girls Club of America, and the United Nations. She led the first known attempt to revamp the quality of presentations for an entire association: the Potent Presentations Initiative for the American Evaluation Association (AEA). She is the 2015 recipient of the AEA's Marcia Guttentag Promising New Evaluator Award, which recognizes early notable and substantial accomplishments in the field. Dr. Evergreen is coeditor and coauthor of two issues of *New Directions for Evaluation* on data visualization. She writes a popular blog on data presentation at StephanieEvergreen.com. The first edition of her book *Presenting Data Effectively: Communicating Your Findings for Maximum Impact* was published by SAGE in the fall of 2013 and was listed as number one in social science research on Amazon in the United States and United Kingdom for several weeks. Her second book, *Effective Data Visualization: The Right Chart for the Right Data,* was published in a Second Edition in May 2019.

INTRODUCTION

WHY SKETCH

"Sure, Stephanie, your idea that good visuals are important is a nice one, but who has that kind of time?" One of the things people always say to me is how long it takes to report. Folks are afraid that designing work well will increase how much time it will take them to produce their report deliverables, and often this imagined extra time is so intimidating that they abandon the notion of well-designed reporting altogether. This sketchbook is here to help you cut down on that prep time.

You do not have to be an artist to sketch. Listen, my drawings look like chicken scratch. At best, I use stick figures and what would appear to onlookers to be blobs. Detailed art is not the point of sketching. The point is simply to make a plan on paper with placeholders for content you'll refine when you are in front of a computer. Only you need to be able to decipher your drawings. You can always find a stock photo, take your own picture, or get a graphic designer to illustrate your ideas later on.

That said, you do not have to sketch alone. Team sketching is a vibrant method for exploring alternatives and coming to consensus. Sketching as a group is one way to elevate the input of those who speak up less often in meetings and provide more overall balance to opinions.

We used to sketch a lot more. Remember professors who drew out their ideas on the chalkboard or free-handed at the overhead projector? Computers replaced our need for live sketching, but that shift came at a cost that research is now uncovering.

In their massive literature review on sketching, Pfister and Eppler[1] culled multiple benefits, including increased memorability. They pointed to outcomes like "knowledge creation, sharing, and documentation" (p. 373), particularly

---

[1]Pfister, R. A., & Eppler, M. J. (2012). The benefits of sketching for knowledge management. *Journal of Knowledge Management, 16*(2), 372–382.

in team-building scenarios and meetings in organizational settings. Sounds good, huh? Schütze, Sachse, and Römer[2] studied the impacts of sketching and found that it helps shorter-term memory processing—it offloads some of the cognitive burden of visualizing content in our mind's eye and frees up our brain space for actual information processing. Their study participants who sketched generated higher-quality answers, too. *And* they said the study task was less difficult than those who did not sketch.

In other words, sketching is good for our brains. Mattison, Dando, and Ormerod[3] studied the impact of sketching on children. Their research showed that children with impaired free-recall memory (i.e., children with autism) were better able to actually recall things they had recently seen when they were allowed to sketch during cognitive interviews. Their responses were 20% more accurate and detailed than those of the control group (children without impaired free recall). Scheiter, Schleinschok, and Ainsworth[4] showed that the more people sketched, the better their learning outcomes on recall and transfer tests. Indeed, sketching has been shown (by Fernandes, Wammes, and Meade[5]) to produce better recall of content across ages, settings, and tasks. Their study reported that drawing no more than four seconds was enough to produce these benefits.

Sketching helps us test ideas. Use pencil! When we sketch, we work through the logical fallacies and errors that would otherwise be embedded in our visuals if we started out in front of a computer. We can iterate designs quickly on paper to minimize the overall time needed to solidify concepts.

Sketching is often a pathway to discovering insights not available at the surface of our thinking. The study produced by Tohidi, Buxton, Baecker, and Sellen[6]

[2]Schütze, M., Sachse, P., & Römer, A. (2003). Support value of sketching in the design process. *Research in Engineering Design, 14,* 89–97.

[3]Mattison, M. L. A., Dando, C. J., & Ormerod, T. C. (2015). Sketching to remember: Episodic free recall task support for child witnesses and victims with autism spectrum disorder. *Journal of Autism Developmental Disorders, 45,* 1751–1765.

[4]Scheiter, K., Schleinschok, K., & Ainsworth, S. (2017). Why sketching may aid learning from science texts: Contrasting sketching with written explanations. *Topics in Cognitive Science, 9,* 866–882.

[5]Fernandes, M. A., Wammes, J. D., & Meade, M. E. (2018). The surprisingly powerful influence of drawing on memory. *Current Directions in Psychological Science, 27*(5), 302–308.

[6]Tohidi, M., Buxton, W., Baecker, R., & Sellen, A. (2006). User sketches: A quick, inexpensive, and effective way to elicit more reflective user feedback. In *Proceedings of the 4th Nordic Conference on Human–Computer Interaction: Changing Roles* (pp. 105–114). New York, NY: ACM.

reported that sketching facilitated reflection and revelation better than conventional methods (aka, just talking things out). You'll get better insights.

Additionally, planning out what your final deliverables will look like now will save you the cognitive energy you'd have had to expend later when crunching your numbers and thinking through your findings. You'll be making skeleton structures now that will be ready and waiting for your final numbers and narrative so that when your data analysis is finished, you can plug and play.

Why sketch? Sketching generates less error, more insights, and maybe even some joy.

WHAT'S AHEAD

This sketchbook is divided into sections, one per project. Within each section, you'll see:

- A Project Profile Page, where you'll list out your main deliverables, related audiences, fonts, colors, and all the other design parameters of your project so you can reference them in one handy place.

- Graph and Dot Grids. Oh yeah, its graph paper, where you can sketch the main graph styles you'll use. You should be able to identify these early in your project, because you already likely know most if not all the metrics you'll be reporting.

- Dashboard Designs on grid paper, where you can rough in a layout for reporting your key indicators, saving you hours of nudging and reorganizing in front of your computer screen.

- One-Page Handout Helpers on grid paper that can double as infographics

- A Slide Guide where you identify your main point (one per slide), quickly sketch the image to support your point, and list out your talking notes so that your on-screen slide construction time is a snap.

- A Report Structure, a place to draw your plans for your report cover and the basic structures for interior and section starter pages, as well as an executive summary.

Each section will provide different options for dashboard and infographic template layouts, so browse through each one along with the examples I've provided from my own projects to see which one most closely aligns with your project needs. If none of those are quite what you are looking for, each section also includes . . .

- Blank pages, where you can dream big.

Together, these sketches will help you develop a consistent, professional look and feel so that everything you produce from this project looks like it belongs together and was generated from someone who knows that high-quality content plus high-impact visual reporting leads to action and decision making.

If you get stuck just staring at a blank page, I'm here to help. First, I'll walk you through an entire project reporting package so you can find some inspiration. Second, on each template page I'll prompt your thinking with insights, tips, and resources. Third, my quantitative and qualitative chart choosers are printed on the inside front and back covers to serve as navigational tools and help you represent your data the clearest. Finally, this book has a hashtag, #evergreensketch—search this hashtag on your favorite social media site, find my sketches and others so you can see how this process looks in action, and get inspired.

SKETCHES FOR A SAMPLE REPORTING PACKAGE

I'll go first.

This project is based on a customer satisfaction survey. The data and related insights will be reported to the senior leaders of this organization, who will use it to make strategic and operational decisions.

PROJECT PROFILE PAGE

Way back when I am first assigned the project, in a moment of down time (haha, I know, just go with it), I complete the Project Profile Page. In many cases, a communications department will dictate the fonts and colors to be used, but this company has only two colors and no condensed font identified, so I fill in the gaps. The company logo is a set of squares, so I'll incorporate squares into the overall design of this project's deliverables.

Resources

I go to **https://coolors.co/** and type the company colors into the first two sections and lock those. Then I hit the space bar on my keyboard to generate color schemes that go with my two colors and keep hitting the space bar until I find a set of colors I like. I can even check how the colors will look to someone who is color-blind. Hovering into the other color swatches reveals their color codes. I jot those down here in my Project Profile Page. (Should Coolors ever break, just search on "color palette generator" and you'll find similar resources.)

To round out the font choices, I either go back to the communications department and ask them for a condensed version of one of the fonts they specified, or I secure permission to swap out the sans serif they provided with a different one that comes in a condensed version. If you have the liberty to pick new fonts, try searching on "condensed" at **https://fonts.google.com**. If you are concerned about picking fonts that will go well together, try searching on one of your fonts at **http://typ.io/**, where you'll see recommended pairings, common descriptors of these fonts' personalities, and how they look in action.

PROJECT PROFILE PAGE

Project Name: Customer Satisfaction Survey

Report Deliverable	Audience	Timing
dashboard	VPs	weekly
slides & handout (possibly)	VPs & higher	quarterly
report	VPs & higher	end of study

Fonts

Heading (sans serif): Roboto

Narrative (serif or sans serif): Merriweather

Condensed (sans serif): Roboto Condensed

Color Codes

Color 1			Color 2			Color 3		
C 91	R 16	HEX	C 100	R 0	HEX	C 0	R 241	HEX
M 38	G 116	1074BC	M 87	G 174	00AEEF	M 46	G 128	F1803C
Y 0	B 188		Y 0	B 239		Y 75	B 60	
K 26	dark blue		K 6	light blue		K 5	orange	

Important Graphic Elements

(icons, navigational guides, shapes inspired by the logo):

VPs like up/down arrows for KPIs

logo has circles so use as data point markers & around icons

Color code & icon sections of slides & handout

Share a snapshot of your project profile page on your favorite social media! #evergreensketch

GRAPH GRIDS

Then, as the project unfolds and I learn what metrics are of most interest to my audience, I sketch out how I might graph the data once they arrive, knowing the frequency at which we are running the survey and the response options we are writing for each question. I use the graph paper to mock up some ideas and run these sketches by my boss to see if the graph form makes sense to her. I get feedback and eventually approval on these formats long before the data are in, so as to cut down on the number of decisions and possible delays during crunch time.

Graphs are where you'll illustrate the visual evidence that supports your main findings related to each metric you are tracking. Use the grid paper to sketch out how you will visualize the data you collect on your main metrics.

Don't know the best chart type to use? Consult the inside front cover for quantitative options. Let's say you want to show the results of a survey. Head to the section called "What the Survey Says" and you'll see a menu of chart choices that best show that kind of data. The inside back cover provides you with options for visualizing qualitative data. Identify the nature of the data you are working with and you'll see dots indicating which visuals can help you showcase that data.

Think carefully about how much detail your particular audience will need. Do they need to see data every month, or is quarterly or yearly sufficient? How many decimal places will they want to see? Will they expect and know how to interpret confidence intervals?

At this stage, you'll be sketching out only the best chart type, given the nature of your data, the number of variables you'll have to show, and your audience's data literacy levels. In the sketches on the next page, your chart titles are likely to be the name of your metric, for example, "Sales Growth." Remember to circle back to the chart's title when you have finished analyzing your data, so you can make the title more meaningful and interpretive, such as "Sales growth dipped in Q2 but rebounded by Q3."

Elevate the story you found in your analysis even further by applying colors to the graphs. Bust out those colored pencils and highlight the parts of the graph that are most germane to your point.

Resources

When it comes time to crank out these sketches digitally, I have posted some introductory step-by-step instructions for building quantitative graphs right in Excel at **https://stephanieevergreen.com/how-to/**.

For step-by-step guidance on building qualitative visuals, head here: **https://stephanieevergreen.com/qualitative-viz/**.

For more in-depth guidance on choosing the best chart type and generating it in Excel, read my book, *Effective Data Visualization*.[7]

---

[7]Evergreen, S. (2019). *Effective data visualization* (2nd ed.). Thousand Oaks, CA: SAGE.

GRAPH GRID

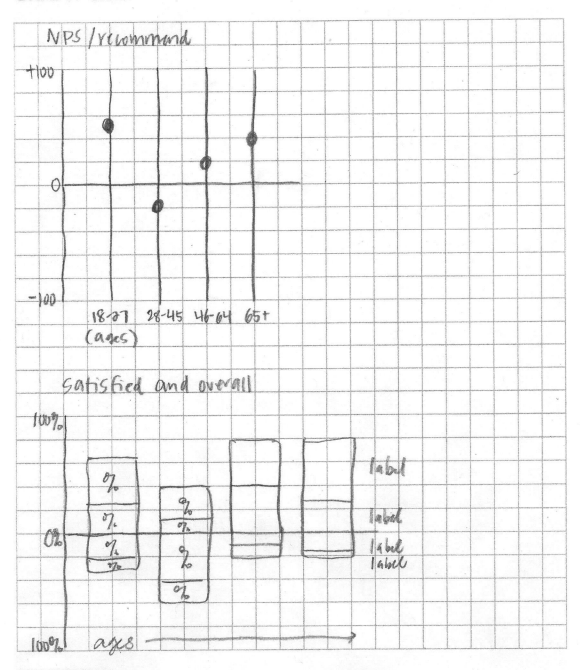

NPS / recommend

+100

0

-100

18-27   28-45   46-64   65+
(ages)

Satisfied and overall

100%

%
%
0%
%
%

%
%
%
%

label
label
label
label

100%   ages

DASHBOARD DESIGN

With the basic graph forms approved, I sketch out how the data could look in a dashboard and run that by my supervisor to make sure I'm planning for the right filters and functionality.

Dashboards are intended to be a one-page document that reports the performance on your key indicators or metrics. They can be a handy guide in giving status updates to busy decision makers about the health of a project. Dashboards tend to lack narrative and context, so they are best suited for an audience that is already familiar with the project.

Use the templates to sketch out how you will lay out your dashboard. You'll find three different dashboard templates in this sketchbook. For my customer satisfaction survey project, I use Dashboard Template A. This particular template design provides space for four quick numbers, three primary graphs, and two larger graphs to house more detailed views. I choose Template A because I have a medium number of metrics to report. Dashboard Template B is for fewer metrics, providing space for six large graphs. Dashboard Template C is for many metrics, where your audience wants to see the raw numbers and you can make tiny snapshots of the trend and comparison data.

Dashboard Template A

Dashboard Template B

In Western cultures, people navigate through documents by starting in the upper left and finishing in the lower right. This means that your dashboard will need to have the highest-priority information in the upper left. From there, people will focus on what's in the top row (think "above the fold" in newspaper terms), with metrics of lesser importance or with greater detail in the bottom row or to the bottom right.

Dashboard Template C

If you plan to allow drill-down into your data, sketch placeholders for filters/slicers near the top of the dashboard.

Even though dashboards do not typically contain much narrative, consider adding just a sentence or two that specifies the purpose of the dashboard and what people should be looking for or doing with the dashboard.

It is a common dashboarding mistake to show data primarily as a large number. While a single large number does give a quick bit of information, most decision makers want a little context to help them know if this number is trending up or down or whether it is close to the goal or far away. Restrict your single big number to just one to four metrics and show the others with their necessary context, such as in a line graph or dumbbell dot plot.

Remember to include a space to indicate when the dashboard was last updated. You don't want people making decisions with dated data.

Resources

Stacey Barr is my top pick for helpful, practical, free advice on choosing the right metrics and organizing them into a dashboard. See her work at **https://www.staceybarr.com/.**

Final dashboard design can be made or broken by the little things, like alignment and tick marks. Check out *Information Dashboard Design* by graphing guru Stephen Few[8] for a nice contrast between weak and solid dashboard designs.

The Big Book of Dashboards[9] is a fun read, not just because it is filled with a wide variety of dashboard examples but also because each featured dashboard is accompanied by a critique of its strengths and weaknesses by the book's editors.

---

[8]Few, S. (2006). *Information dashboard design: The effective visual communication of data*. Sebastopol, CA: O'Reilly.

[9]Wexler, S., Shaffer, J., & Cotgreave, A. (2017). *The big book of dashboards*. Hoboken, NJ: Wiley.

DASHBOARD DESIGN A

Title: Customer Satisfaction Survey

Filters: gender, race, income, age

Introductory Sentences: We ran a survey of all customers at the end of their help call.

Last Updated:

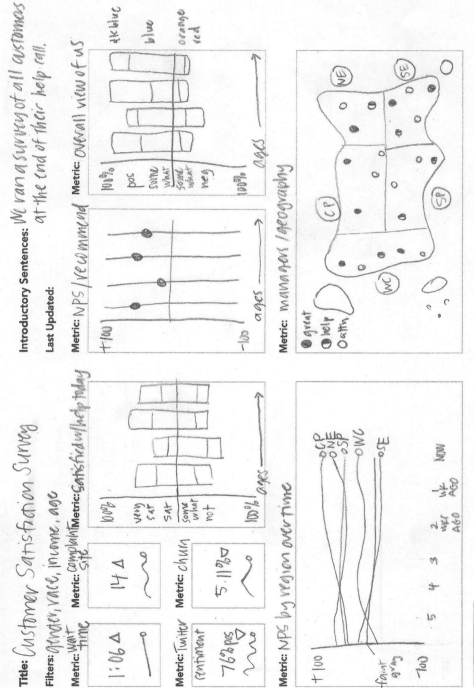

Metric: Wait time — 1:06 △

Metric: Complaint site — 14 △

Metric: Satisfied w/ help today
100% ... very sat / sat / somewhat / not — ages

Metric: Twitter sentiment — 762 pos △

Metric: churn — 5.11% △

Metric: NPS / recommend
+100 / -100 — ages

Metric: Overall view of us
100% pos / somewhat / somewhat / neg / 100% — ages
dk/blue, blue, orange, red

Metric: NPS by region over time
+100 / front giving / -100
5 4 3 2 wks ago / wk ago / NOW
CP, NE, SP, WC, SE

Metric: main areas / geography
great / help / calm
NE, SE, CP, SP, WC

#evergreensketch

13

REPORT STRUCTURE

Reports are designed to be a platform where you dive into the details of your work, describing the insights you discovered and the evidence that supports them. Most people will also narrate things like action items, conclusions, and methods used in data collection and analysis.

At this point, I can also sketch out what our report structure will look like. I don't need the actual data to plan out what imagery we will use and where specific blocks of text will go. I use this as an opportunity to think about which colors could go where to support engagement without distracting. This one doesn't reveal any real or mock data, so I post a picture of this to Instagram, tagging it with #evergreensketch.

I often recommend the 1-3-25 reporting approach, where you have a one-page handout (templates provided), a three-page executive summary, and a 25-page report (with as many appendices as you'd like). This approach is a way to guarantee that you'll have a report with a level of detail that meets your audience where they are, wherever they are, without overloading them with so many details that they'll just stop engaging.

In keeping with a "bottom line up front" reporting orientation, you'll prioritize your findings, conclusions, and action items in the 25-page report and relegate most of the technical discussion of methods to the appendices.

The report structure has a place for you to sketch your three-page executive summary. It should have data-based visuals. You'll also see places to sketch key pages of your longer report: the cover, an internal section start page, and an internal narrative page.

The rule of thirds can also help the development of these pages, where you might have one-third of your page taken up by a sidebar to hold a case study. Or it might be blank so your page has some breathing room.

Sometimes long reports are unavoidable. You can help your readers quickly access the content they are seeking by implementing some navigational tools. Think about assigning icons or strips of color to each section, perhaps hyperlinked from the table of contents, so your readers can jump to what they came to read.

Resources

If you struggle to know what your funder really wants to see in your report, check out this guidance document I developed in collaboration with the Ewing Marion Kauffman Foundation: **https://www.kauffman.org/evaluation/ evaluation-reporting-guide**. Working with funders enlightened me about what they are keen to see in a report, and I'm sure it'll help you, too.

My book *Presenting Data Effectively*[10] has loads of examples of great reports.

Of course, reporting out our data does not always come in the form of a PDF or a web page. Kylie Hutchinson has fun ideas for sharing data and insights in her book *Innovative Evaluation Reporting*.[11]

---

[10]Evergreen, S. (2018). *Presenting data effectively*. Thousand Oaks, CA: SAGE.

[11]Hutchinson, K. (2018). *A short primer on innovative evaluation reporting*. Gibsons, BC, Canada: Author.

REPORT STRUCTURE

Executive Summary page 1

Customer Sat Q1

○ WHAT

NPS & POC

Analysis of Transcripts

DATA COLLECTION
- Survey of X, Y %
- post call
- tends to get love or hate
— Sidebar

heat map of themes
x sampled calls

Executive Summary page 2

(blank)

○ SO WHAT

[insert HR section on hiring]
- impacts (expected in 3 months)
[comms report]
  - mistrust
  - trust

CEO's words
[insert new message]
~ ~
— Sidebar

(arrow) cons

Executive Summary page 3

(blank)

○ NOW WHAT

Monitoring Plan
- random samples of calls - 18 mo.
- internal message
- SVP of Inclusion, CEO
etc.

CONTACT INFO
- us
- boss
- HR
- comms
- CEO

Logo

Report cover page

(blank)

WHAT INCLUSION LOOKS LIKE HERE — working title

photo - Cannot be smiling diverse stock photo

contact info
date of pub

Logo

Section starter page

(blank)

(icon)

WHAT
define section
define problem
show metrics

Internal page

○ WHAT
icon!

Heading
~ ~

graphs

highlight passages

EXAMPLE TRANSCRIPT
~
~
~
~

#evergreensketch

SLIDE GUIDE

Then the data come in and I put down the sketchbook for a while to explore, analyze, and think. Once I have some insights to share with senior management, I start planning the slideshow. The issue surfacing in the data is that middle-income people of color are reporting dissatisfaction, though other demographic groups are generally satisfied. Aside from the graphs, what imagery would I want to include in the slides? I have many choices here. I could include real photos of our actual customers to help decision makers keep them front of mind. I could include imagery related to our initial plans to listen in on calls to our technical support center and sketch out blobs that resemble (at least in my mind) a photo series of headsets and cell phones. I could work in icons that represent our problem-solving approach. In reality, decisions about the direction of the imagery often come down to budget and time constraints as well as access to photos that are accurate and representational.

Slideshows are used as a visual backbone, to support the speaker with visuals that mirror the content they are delivering verbally.

The best slideshows do not contain all the words the speaker will say, which strains the audience's cognition (and patience). The best slideshows are mainly pictures. Use the slide guide on the next page to write out your main point for each slide and sketch what visual you'll use to support that point. Then jot a few notes for your talking points on each slide.

Consider adapting the rule of thirds as a structure for each slide. With this structure, you divide your slide into three rows and three columns. You'll put your main point in one row and your visual support in the other two. Or you'll put your main point in one column and your visual support in the other two. Or you'll fill all three thirds with your visual support and you'll pop a text box on top to hold your main point in one of the thirds. This structure guarantees that your slides will look consistent and organized across your entire deck.

It may not be realistic for you to make every slide a large picture. That's okay. You will want pictures on the slides that are there to compel action in the audience. You'll also want a picture on the cover slide so that people are visually engaged as they walk into the presentation room. Use the slide guide to flesh out those slides.

You may have heard people suggest that you should "storyboard" your presentation. This means, simply, that you plan out the order of your slides so you can see how you'll progress through your content. What will be your logical first topic? Your second? Let me recommend a winning idea: Give people the bottom line up front. This is what they came to hear. Hook them in with a big reveal.

Resources

Great slides shouldn't be able to stand alone. They should need you there to provide the valuable content. If you need help convincing people (including yourself) that the slides should not be your handout, read up: **https://stephanie evergreen.com/stop-asking-if-the-slides-are-available/**.

For more examples of great-looking slides and details on how to use PowerPoint to construct them, check out my book *Presenting Data Effectively*.[12]

Garr Reynolds is the person who taught me about storyboarding and opened my eyes to what great presentations can do for you. His book *Presentation Zen*[13] is a timeless classic, and his website (**https://www.presentationzen .com/**) is full of ideas.

---

[12]Evergreen, S. (2018). *Presenting data effectively*. Thousand Oaks, CA: SAGE.

[13]Reynolds, G. (2008). *Presentation zen*. Berkeley, CA: New Riders.

SLIDE GUIDE

Headline: Survey Results!

Customer Satisfaction Q1

Talking Points: how & when we collected

Headline: but wait time is ↑

Talking Points: Animate regions & discuss trends

Headline: Call center sat ↓

Talking Points: Esp. w/ people of color, consistent over last few periods

---

Headline: agenda

WHAT — mag glass
SO WHAT — story
NOW WHAT — keys

Talking Points: what we know, what it means, what to do

Headline: web complaints ↑

wait — web

Talking Points: Correlates w/wait time historically, leads to losses

---

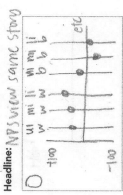

Headline: NPS view same story

+100 / -100
ul mi li
w w b b L etc

Talking Points: break down by income, pinpoint unhappiest group

---

Headline: NPS - Some regions are high

+100 / wc / -100

what icon

Talking Points: Steady in some areas

Headline: Twitter sentiment ↓

hostile / disapp / neutral / finust / amused

color match WHAT icon

Talking Points: weekly analysis shows shift toward negative

Headline: So what

HOW DOES THIS IMPACT THE ORG?

So what icon

Talking Points: moral, clinical, financial considerations

#evergreensketch

19

ONE-PAGE HANDOUT HELPER

One-page handouts are a digestible, condensed form of your most important points and action items. They are incredibly useful accompaniments to a presentation, the birthplace of your web page content, or a more respectable alternative to an infographic.

Given the insights my team saw in the data and the plan of action we identified with our supervisor, I have the materials to generate a What/So What/Now What framework for a handout that will accompany the slideshow. It relies on colors, fonts, and graphic elements that I identified months ago, saving me loads of time and freeing up my brain space so I can focus on clear, informative content.

Like the dashboard, your one-page handout should be organized to align with a top-to-bottom, left-to-right reading culture.

You'll see three variations of handout templates in this sketchbook. All templates provide space for an informative title and a few sentences of narrative at the top and contact details and a logo in the lower right, within the gray bar. Template A is set up around three main topic areas, with two subpoints for each of those main topic areas, giving you space for six visuals. Template B prioritizes one main point but gives space for three secondary points and a location to spell out a recommendation or a call to action. Template C features three main points, where you'll have a little more room to elaborate with narrative, and placeholders for icons that will relate to each point. My customer satisfaction project is shaping up to be a What/So What/Now What structure, which is three points, so I'll go with Template C.

Unlike the dashboard, a one-page handout has a balance between narrative and visuals. Use the narrative to tell a story and the visuals to provide the evidence for your story.

Feel free to combine the space for two visuals into one larger visual if you have a graph with a lot of data that simply needs more space to be seen clearly.

Pay close attention to the titles of those visuals, since that is where you'll weave your story. In fact, the topic headings themselves should be more like headlines that make a statement.

Your visuals here can be quantitative or qualitative, of course. Indeed, it is the blend of the two that tends to be most convincing to audiences.

Alignment of the elements within the one-page handout is critical. Spaces for the visuals need to be the same size and they need to fill the space of an entire cell in this grid, lining up exactly with the other elements in the handout.

Handout Template A

Handout Template B

Handout Template C

When things don't line up, the handout comes off looking sloppy and amateur, and that is not you.

Resources

Check out this one-pager makeover to see how updates to titles and visuals tell a stronger story: **https://stephanieevergreen.com/easy-simple-one-page-handout/**.

I make a one-page handout of my own personal success metrics each year. Read my 2018 Personal Annual Report for more ideas about how to report on a lot of metrics in one space: **https://stephanieevergreen.com/my-2018-personal-annual-report**.

ONE PAGE HANDOUT HELPER C

Title: Customer Satisfaction Survey shows decline among key groups.

A few introductory sentences: We survey after every call (when consent) & analyze data weekly. Recent trends indicate... Survey questions are...

Icon 1
WHAT
magnifying glass

Main point 1: Overall view of company ↓ in some areas, esp. w/ middle income people of color located in Southeast.

Main Point 1 Graph: % pos & somewhat pos middle income POC

100%

0% WC NE SP CP SE

(lollipop graph)

Icon 2
SO WHAT
ripple

Main point 2: Likely to impact other areas. Downward trend in recent months predicts loss of $ /mo.

Main Point 2 Graph: % pos & somewhat pos

100%

0% Q4 Q1 Q2 Q3 Q4 Now

o MI WSE
o UI BSE
. etc.

Icon 3
NOW WHAT
Keys

Main point 3: Proposed action plan - collect equal data from help calls & analyze

Main Point 3 Graph: possible actions

① listen in   ② POC analysts on transcripts   ③ reconvene w/ more data

---

Call to Action/Conclusion: Still can turn this around w/ commitment to change

Contact info: Stephanie ...

Logo:

This sketching process saves mental space and stress by offloading some critical decisions to noncritical times and creating a visual plan of action. Our sketched plans might have to be adjusted once we have actual data, but the expense is small compared to the cost of staring at a blank page while deadlines knock at your door.

You certainly do not have to use every template in each section for all projects. Some of my projects include only a report and a dashboard. Pick and choose what works best for you or use the wide-open sketch areas to invent a new template that fits you even better. And let us see it! Post a pic with #evergreensketch.

SKETCH TEMPLATES FOR PROJECT 1

PROJECT PROFILE PAGE

Project Name:

Report Deliverable	Audience	Timing

Fonts

Heading (sans serif):

Narrative (serif or sans serif):

Condensed (sans serif):

Color Codes

Color 1			Color 2			Color 3		
C	R	HEX	C	R	HEX	C	R	HEX
M	G		M	G		M	G	
Y	B		Y	B		Y	B	
K			K			K		

Important Graphic Elements

(icons, navigational guides, shapes inspired by the logo):

Share a snapshot of your project profile page on your favorite social media! #evergreensketch

GRAPH GRID A

#evergreensketch

GRAPH GRID B

#evergreensketch

DASHBOARD DESIGN A

Title:

Filters:

Introductory Sentences:

Last Updated:

Metric:

Metric:

Metric:

Metric:

Metric:

Metric:

Metric:

Metric:

Metric:

DASHBOARD DESIGN B

Title:

Filters:

Introductory Sentences:

Last Updated:

Metric:

Metric:

Metric:

Metric:

Metric:

Metric:

DASHBOARD DESIGN C

Title:

Filters:

Introductory Sentences:

Last Updated:

Metric Name	Q1	Q2	Q3	Q4	Q1	Trendline	Q/Q Diff	Target	Current Q v. Target	Notes

#evergreensketch

ONE-PAGE HANDOUT HELPER A

Title:

A few introductory sentences:

Main point 1:

Headline for Graph 1A:

Graph 1A:

Headline for Graph 1B:

Graph 1B:

Main point 2:

Headline for Graph 2A:

Graph 2A:

Headline for Graph 2B:

Graph 2B:

Main point 3:

Headline for Graph 3A:

Graph 3A:

Headline for Graph 3B:

Graph 3B:

Contact info:

Logo:

#evergreensketch

ONE-PAGE HANDOUT HELPER B

Title:

A few introductory sentences:

Main point:

Main Point Graph:

Subpoint 1:

Subpoint 1 Graph:

Subpoint 2:

Subpoint 2 Graph:

Subpoint 3:

Subpoint 3 Graph:

Call to Action:

Contact info:

Logo:

#evergreensketch

ONE-PAGE HANDOUT HELPER C

Title:

A few introductory sentences:

Icon 1

Main point 1:

Main Point 1 Graph:

Icon 2

Main point 2:

Main Point 2 Graph:

Icon 3

Main point 3:

Main Point 3 Graph:

Call to Action/Conclusion:

Contact info:

Logo:

#evergreensketch

Headline:

Talking Points:

Headline:

Talking Points:

Headline:

Talking Points:

Headline:

Talking Points:

Headline:

Talking Points:

Headline:

Talking Points:

Headline:

Talking Points:

Headline:

Talking Points:

Headline:

Talking Points:

#evergreensketch

REPORT STRUCTURE

Executive Summary page 1

Executive Summary page 2

Executive Summary page 3

Report cover page

Section starter page

Internal page

NOTES

SKETCH TEMPLATES FOR PROJECT 2

PROJECT PROFILE PAGE

Project Name:

Report Deliverable	Audience	Timing

Fonts

Heading (sans serif):

Narrative (serif or sans serif):

Condensed (sans serif):

Color Codes

Color 1			Color 2			Color 3		
C	R	HEX	C	R	HEX	C	R	HEX
M	G		M	G		M	G	
Y	B		Y	B		Y	B	
K			K			K		

Important Graphic Elements

(icons, navigational guides, shapes inspired by the logo):

GRAPH GRID A

#evergreensketch

GRAPH GRID B

DASHBOARD DESIGN A

Title:

Filters:

Introductory Sentences:

Last Updated:

Metric:

Metric:

Metric:

Metric:

Metric:

Metric:

Metric:

Metric:

DASHBOARD DESIGN B

Title:

Filters:

Introductory Sentences:

Last Updated:

Metric:

Metric:

Metric:

Metric:

Metric:

Metric:

DASHBOARD DESIGN C

Title:

Filters:

Introductory Sentences:

Last Updated:

Metric Name	Q1	Q2	Q3	Q4	Q1	Trendline	Q/Q Diff	Target	Current Q v. Target	Notes

ONE-PAGE HANDOUT HELPER A

Title:

A few introductory sentences:

Main point 1:

Headline for Graph 1A:

Graph 1A:

Headline for Graph 1B:

Graph 1B:

Main point 2:

Headline for Graph 2A:

Graph 2A:

Headline for Graph 2B:

Graph 2B:

Main point 3:

Headline for Graph 3A:

Graph 3A:

Headline for Graph 3B:

Graph 3B:

Contact info:

Logo:

#evergreensketch

ONE-PAGE HANDOUT HELPER B

Title:

A few introductory sentences:

Main point:

Main Point Graph:

Subpoint 1:

Subpoint 1 Graph:

Subpoint 2:

Subpoint 2 Graph:

Subpoint 3:

Subpoint 3 Graph:

Call to Action:

Contact info:

Logo:

#evergreensketch

ONE-PAGE HANDOUT HELPER C

Title:

A few introductory sentences:

Icon 1

Main point 1:

Main Point 1 Graph:

Icon 2

Main point 2:

Main Point 2 Graph:

Icon 3

Main point 3:

Main Point 3 Graph:

Call to Action/Conclusion:

Contact info:

Logo:

Headline:

Talking Points:

Headline:

Talking Points:

Headline:

Talking Points:

Headline:

Talking Points:

Headline:

Talking Points:

Headline:

Talking Points:

Headline:

Talking Points:

Headline:

Talking Points:

Headline:

Talking Points:

#evergreensketch

REPORT STRUCTURE

Executive Summary page 1

Executive Summary page 2

Executive Summary page 3

Report cover page

Section starter page

Internal page

NOTES

SKETCH TEMPLATES FOR PROJECT 3

PROJECT PROFILE PAGE

Project Name:

Report Deliverable	Audience	Timing

Fonts

Heading (sans serif):

Narrative (serif or sans serif):

Condensed (sans serif):

Color Codes

Color 1			Color 2			Color 3		
C	R	HEX	C	R	HEX	C	R	HEX
M	G		M	G		M	G	
Y	B		Y	B		Y	B	
K			K			K		

Important Graphic Elements

(icons, navigational guides, shapes inspired by the logo):

Share a snapshot of your project profile page on your favorite social media! #evergreensketch

GRAPH GRID A

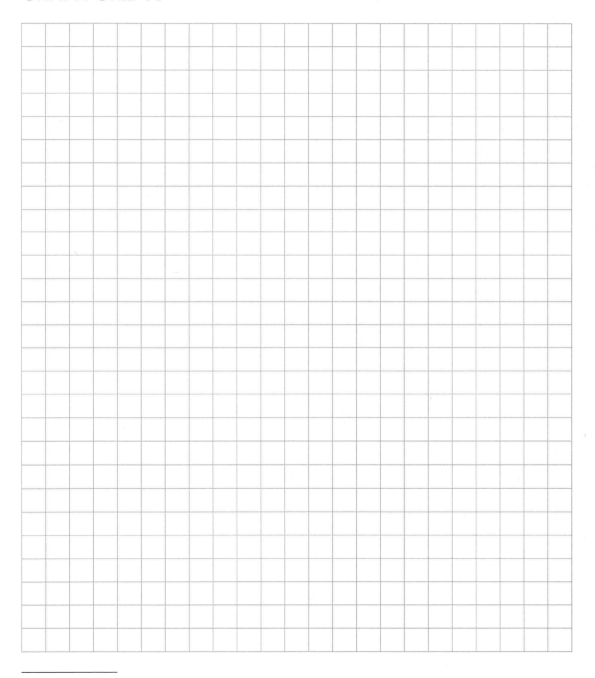

GRAPH GRID B

#evergreensketch

DASHBOARD DESIGN A

Title:

Filters:

Metric:

Metric:

Metric:

Metric:

Metric:

Metric:

Introductory Sentences:

Last Updated:

Metric:

Metric:

Metric:

Metric:

DASHBOARD DESIGN B

Title:

Filters:

Introductory Sentences:

Last Updated:

Metric:

Metric:

Metric:

Metric:

Metric:

Metric:

DASHBOARD DESIGN C

Title:

Filters:

Introductory Sentences:

Last Updated:

Metric Name	Q1	Q2	Q3	Q4	Q1	Trendline	Q/Q Diff	Target	Current Q v. Target	Notes

#evergreensketch

ONE-PAGE HANDOUT HELPER A

Title:

A few introductory sentences:

Main point 1:

Headline for Graph 1A:	Headline for Graph 1B:
Graph 1A:	Graph 1B:

Main point 2:

Headline for Graph 2A:	Headline for Graph 2B:
Graph 2A:	Graph 2B:

Main point 3:

Headline for Graph 3A:	Headline for Graph 3B:
Graph 3A:	Graph 3B:

Contact info: **Logo:**

#evergreensketch

ONE-PAGE HANDOUT HELPER B

Title:

A few introductory sentences:

Main point:

Main Point Graph:

Subpoint 1:

Subpoint 2:

Subpoint 3:

Subpoint 1 Graph:

Subpoint 2 Graph:

Subpoint 3 Graph:

Call to Action:

Contact info:

Logo:

#evergreensketch

ONE-PAGE HANDOUT HELPER C

Title:

A few introductory sentences:

Icon 1

Main point 1:

Main Point 1 Graph:

Icon 2

Main point 2:

Main Point 2 Graph:

Icon 3

Main point 3:

Main Point 3 Graph:

Call to Action/Conclusion:

Contact info:

Logo:

#evergreensketch

Headline:

Talking Points:

Headline:

Talking Points:

Headline:

Talking Points:

Headline:

Talking Points:

Headline:

Talking Points:

Headline:

Talking Points:

Headline:

Talking Points:

Headline:

Talking Points:

Headline:

Talking Points:

#evergreensketch

REPORT STRUCTURE

Executive Summary page 1

Executive Summary page 2

Executive Summary page 3

Report cover page

Section starter page

Internal page

NOTES

SKETCH TEMPLATES FOR PROJECT 4

PROJECT PROFILE PAGE

Project Name:

Report Deliverable	Audience	Timing

Fonts

Heading (sans serif):

Narrative (serif or sans serif):

Condensed (sans serif):

Color Codes

Color 1			Color 2			Color 3		
C	R	HEX	C	R	HEX	C	R	HEX
M	G		M	G		M	G	
Y	B		Y	B		Y	B	
K			K			K		

Important Graphic Elements

(icons, navigational guides, shapes inspired by the logo):

GRAPH GRID A

#evergreensketch

GRAPH GRID B

#evergreensketch

DASHBOARD DESIGN A

Title:

Filters:

Metric:

Metric:

Metric:

Metric:

Metric:

Metric:

Introductory Sentences:

Last Updated:

Metric:

Metric:

Metric:

Metric:

DASHBOARD DESIGN B

Title:

Filters:

Introductory Sentences:

Last Updated:

Metric:

Metric:

Metric:

Metric:

Metric:

Metric:

#evergreensketch

DASHBOARD DESIGN C

Title:

Filters:

Introductory Sentences:

Last Updated:

Metric Name	Q1	Q2	Q3	Q4	Q1	Trendline	Q/Q Diff	Target	Current Q v. Target	Notes

ONE-PAGE HANDOUT HELPER A

Title:

A few introductory sentences:

Main point 1:

Headline for Graph 1A:

Graph 1A:

Headline for Graph 1B:

Graph 1B:

Main point 2:

Headline for Graph 2A:

Graph 2A:

Headline for Graph 2B:

Graph 2B:

Main point 3:

Headline for Graph 3A:

Graph 3A:

Headline for Graph 3B:

Graph 3B:

Contact info: **Logo:**

#evergreensketch

ONE-PAGE HANDOUT HELPER B

Title:

A few introductory sentences:

Main point:

Main Point Graph:

Subpoint 1:

Subpoint 2:

Subpoint 3:

Subpoint 1 Graph:

Subpoint 2 Graph:

Subpoint 3 Graph:

Call to Action:

Contact info:

Logo:

#evergreensketch

ONE-PAGE HANDOUT HELPER C

Title:

A few introductory sentences:

Icon 1

Main point 1:

Main Point 1 Graph:

Icon 2

Main point 2:

Main Point 2 Graph:

Icon 3

Main point 3:

Main Point 3 Graph:

Call to Action/Conclusion:

Contact info:

Logo:

#evergreensketch

Headline:

Talking Points:

Headline:

Talking Points:

Headline:

Talking Points:

Headline:

Talking Points:

Headline:

Talking Points:

Headline:

Talking Points:

Headline:

Talking Points:

Headline:

Talking Points:

Headline:

Talking Points:

REPORT STRUCTURE

Executive Summary page 1

Executive Summary page 2

Executive Summary page 3

Report cover page

Section starter page

Internal page

NOTES

SKETCH TEMPLATES FOR PROJECT 5

PROJECT PROFILE PAGE

Project Name:

Report Deliverable	Audience	Timing

Fonts

Heading (sans serif):

Narrative (serif or sans serif):

Condensed (sans serif):

Color Codes

Color 1			Color 2			Color 3		
C	R	HEX	C	R	HEX	C	R	HEX
M	G		M	G		M	G	
Y	B		Y	B		Y	B	
K			K			K		

Important Graphic Elements

(icons, navigational guides, shapes inspired by the logo):

Share a snapshot of your project profile page on your favorite social media! #evergreensketch

GRAPH GRID A

GRAPH GRID B

DASHBOARD DESIGN A

Title:

Filters:

Introductory Sentences:

Last Updated:

Metric:

Metric:

Metric:

Metric:

Metric:

Metric:

Metric:

Metric:

#evergreensketch

DASHBOARD DESIGN B

Title:

Filters:

Introductory Sentences:

Last Updated:

Metric:

Metric:

Metric:

Metric:

Metric:

Metric:

DASHBOARD DESIGN C

Title:

Filters:

Introductory Sentences:

Last Updated:

Metric Name	Q1	Q2	Q3	Q4	Q1	Trendline	Q/Q Diff	Target	Current Q v. Target	Notes

ONE-PAGE HANDOUT HELPER A

Title:

A few introductory sentences:

Main point 1:

Headline for Graph 1A:

Graph 1A:

Headline for Graph 1B:

Graph 1B:

Main point 2:

Headline for Graph 2A:

Graph 2A:

Headline for Graph 2B:

Graph 2B:

Main point 3:

Headline for Graph 3A:

Graph 3A:

Headline for Graph 3B:

Graph 3B:

Contact info:

Logo:

#evergreensketch

ONE-PAGE HANDOUT HELPER B

Title:

A few introductory sentences:

Main point:

Main Point Graph:

Subpoint 1:

Subpoint 2:

Subpoint 3:

Subpoint 1 Graph:

Subpoint 2 Graph:

Subpoint 3 Graph:

Call to Action:

Contact info:

Logo:

#evergreensketch

ONE-PAGE HANDOUT HELPER C

Title:

A few introductory sentences:

Icon 1

Main point 1:

Main Point 1 Graph:

Icon 2

Main point 2:

Main Point 2 Graph:

Icon 3

Main point 3:

Main Point 3 Graph:

Call to Action/Conclusion:

Contact info:

Logo:

#evergreensketch

Headline:

Talking Points:

Headline:

Talking Points:

Headline:

Talking Points:

Headline:

Talking Points:

Headline:

Talking Points:

Headline:

Talking Points:

Headline:

Talking Points:

Headline:

Talking Points:

Headline:

Talking Points:

REPORT STRUCTURE

Executive Summary page 1

Executive Summary page 2

Executive Summary page 3

Report cover page

Section starter page

Internal page

NOTES

SKETCH TEMPLATES FOR PROJECT 6

PROJECT PROFILE PAGE

Project Name:

Report Deliverable	Audience	Timing

Fonts

Heading (sans serif):

Narrative (serif or sans serif):

Condensed (sans serif):

Color Codes

Color 1			Color 2			Color 3		
C	R	HEX	C	R	HEX	C	R	HEX
M	G		M	G		M	G	
Y	B		Y	B		Y	B	
K			K			K		

Important Graphic Elements

(icons, navigational guides, shapes inspired by the logo):

Share a snapshot of your project profile page on your favorite social media! #evergreensketch

GRAPH GRID A

#evergreensketch

GRAPH GRID B

#evergreensketch

DASHBOARD DESIGN A

Title:

Filters:

Metric:

Metric:

Metric:

Metric:

Introductory Sentences:

Last Updated:

Metric:

Metric:

Metric:

Metric:

Metric:

DASHBOARD DESIGN B

Title:

Filters:

Introductory Sentences:

Last Updated:

Metric:

Metric:

Metric:

Metric:

Metric:

Metric:

DASHBOARD DESIGN C

Title:

Filters:

Introductory Sentences:

Last Updated:

Metric Name	Q1	Q2	Q3	Q4	Q1	Trendline	Q/Q Diff	Target	Current Q v. Target	Notes

#evergreensketch

ONE-PAGE HANDOUT HELPER A

Title:

A few introductory sentences:

Main point 1:

Headline for Graph 1A:	Headline for Graph 1B:
Graph 1A:	Graph 1B:

Main point 2:

Headline for Graph 2A:	Headline for Graph 2B:
Graph 2A:	Graph 2B:

Main point 3:

Headline for Graph 3A:	Headline for Graph 3B:
Graph 3A:	Graph 3B:

Contact info: Logo:

#evergreensketch

ONE-PAGE HANDOUT HELPER B

Title:

A few introductory sentences:

Main point:

Main Point Graph:

Subpoint 1:

Subpoint 2:

Subpoint 3:

Subpoint 1 Graph:

Subpoint 2 Graph:

Subpoint 3 Graph:

Call to Action:

Contact info:

Logo:

#evergreensketch

ONE-PAGE HANDOUT HELPER C

Title:

A few introductory sentences:

Icon 1

Main point 1:

Main Point 1 Graph:

Icon 2

Main point 2:

Main Point 2 Graph:

Icon 3

Main point 3:

Main Point 3 Graph:

Call to Action/Conclusion:

Contact info:

Logo:

#evergreensketch

Headline:

Talking Points:

Headline:

Talking Points:

Headline:

Talking Points:

Headline:

Talking Points:

Headline:

Talking Points:

Headline:

Talking Points:

Headline:

Talking Points:

Headline:

Talking Points:

Headline:

Talking Points:

#evergreensketch

REPORT STRUCTURE

Executive Summary page 1

Executive Summary page 2

Executive Summary page 3

Report cover page

Section starter page

Internal page

NOTES

SKETCH TEMPLATES FOR PROJECT 7

PROJECT PROFILE PAGE

Project Name:

Report Deliverable	Audience	Timing

Fonts

Heading (sans serif):

Narrative (serif or sans serif):

Condensed (sans serif):

Color Codes

Color 1			Color 2			Color 3		
C	R	HEX	C	R	HEX	C	R	HEX
M	G		M	G		M	G	
Y	B		Y	B		Y	B	
K			K			K		

Important Graphic Elements

(icons, navigational guides, shapes inspired by the logo):

Share a snapshot of your project profile page on your favorite social media! #evergreensketch

GRAPH GRID A

GRAPH GRID B

DASHBOARD DESIGN A

Title:

Filters:

Introductory Sentences:

Last Updated:

Metric:

Metric:

Metric:

Metric:

Metric:

Metric:

Metric:

Metric:

Metric:

DASHBOARD DESIGN B

Title:

Filters:

Introductory Sentences:

Last Updated:

Metric:

Metric:

Metric:

Metric:

Metric:

Metric:

#evergreensketch

DASHBOARD DESIGN C

Title:

Filters:

Introductory Sentences:

Last Updated:

Metric Name	Q1	Q2	Q3	Q4	Q1	Trendline	Q/Q Diff	Target	Current Q v. Target	Notes

#evergreensketch

ONE-PAGE HANDOUT HELPER A

Title:

A few introductory sentences:

Main point 1:

Headline for Graph 1A:

Graph 1A:

Headline for Graph 1B:

Graph 1B:

Main point 2:

Headline for Graph 2A:

Graph 2A:

Headline for Graph 2B:

Graph 2B:

Main point 3:

Headline for Graph 3A:

Graph 3A:

Headline for Graph 3B:

Graph 3B:

Contact info:

Logo:

#evergreensketch

ONE-PAGE HANDOUT HELPER B

Title:

A few introductory sentences:

Main point:

Main Point Graph:

Subpoint 1:

Subpoint 1 Graph:

Subpoint 2:

Subpoint 2 Graph:

Subpoint 3:

Subpoint 3 Graph:

Call to Action:

Contact info:

Logo:

#evergreensketch

ONE-PAGE HANDOUT HELPER C

Title:

A few introductory sentences:

Icon 1

Main point 1:

Main Point 1 Graph:

Icon 2

Main point 2:

Main Point 2 Graph:

Icon 3

Main point 3:

Main Point 3 Graph:

Call to Action/Conclusion:

Contact info:

Logo:

#evergreensketch

Headline:

Talking Points:

Headline:

Talking Points:

Headline:

Talking Points:

Headline:

Talking Points:

Headline:

Talking Points:

Headline:

Talking Points:

Headline:

Talking Points:

Headline:

Talking Points:

Headline:

Talking Points:

#evergreensketch

119

REPORT STRUCTURE

Executive Summary page 1

Executive Summary page 2

Executive Summary page 3

Report cover page

Section starter page

Internal page

NOTES

I sketched this sketchbook, if you want to see how meta this can get.

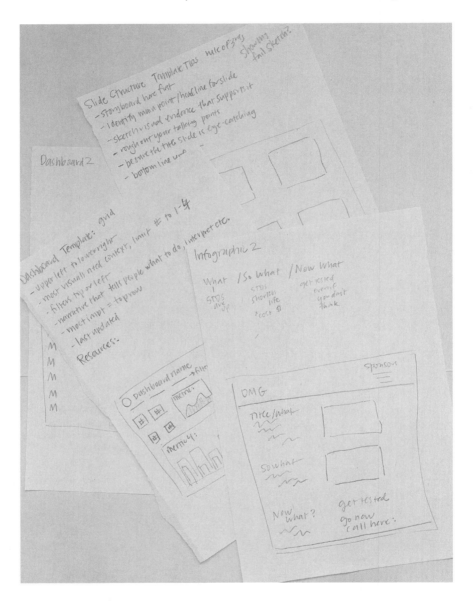

A blank Word document shining in my face makes me want to go clean my office or find a million ways to procrastinate getting started. But sitting down with paper and pencil is less intimidating. I'm more open to thinking through multiple options when I'm sketching. I'm more creative. I feel more prepared when I'm done. Sketching is where the juice is.